ADOLESCENTS

AND

ADD

Gaining the Advantage

Patricia O. Quinn, M.D.

Magination Press ◆ New York

Boro Park

Library of Congress Cataloging-in-Publication Data

Quinn, Patricia O.
 Adolescents and ADD : gaining the advantage / Patricia O. Quinn.
  p.   cm.
 Includes bibliographical references (p.).
 Summary: Addresses the particular concerns of adolescents
diagnosed with attention deficit disorder and offers coping
strategies as well as personal stories from teens with the disorder.
 ISBN 0-945354-70-3
  1. Attention-deficit-disordered youth—Education (Secondary)—
United States—Juvenile literature.   2. Attention-deficit
hyperactivity disorder—United States—Juvenile literature.
[1. Attention-deficit hyperactivity disorder.] I. Title.
LC4713.4.Q56   1995
371.94—dc20   95-25301
                                                              CIP
                                                               AC

Copyright 1995 © by Patricia O. Quinn

Cover photograph by Susan Hur
Cover design by Brigid McCarthy

Published by
MAGINATION PRESS
an Imprint of Brunner/Mazel, Inc.
19 Union Square West
New York, NY 10003

Manufactured in the United States of America

10 9 8 7 6 5 4 3 2

10/15/96

TABLE OF CONTENTS

INTRODUCTION

Congratulations! You have made it. You are now either a middle school or high school student. This book is for all adolescents with Attention Deficit Disorder (ADD): those who have recently been diagnosed and those who have been living with it for some time but now find themselves struggling as they try to cope with a more complicated school schedule and the other demands of being a teenager. We hope this book will give you a better understanding of your attention disorder and provide some valuable hints to help you achieve success.

Other students are going through these same experiences and have fears and disappointments just like yours. All of the students who speak to you in this book have been diagnosed with ADD. They have a good idea of what you are going through at this time in your life and speak to you about their own experiences and solutions.

Adolescence provides many challenges, but you should always remember that there are people willing to help you. These include your parents, coaches, teachers, counselors, tutors, older brothers and sisters, and various health professionals (nurses, physicians, psychologists, and psychiatrists). They, as well as all the contributors to this book, want you to succeed and enjoy these wonderful years.

1.♦
SO YOU HAVE ADD

Adolescence is an exciting time. You have more freedom and enjoy being with your friends. There are other changes as well. You have to cope with many new situations, such as dating, going to parties, getting an after-school job, or playing varsity sports, which usually means practicing every day. The work at school also seems to be getting harder, and the teachers are more demanding.

These changes can be very difficult for *any* student but are more so for students with Attention Deficit Disorder (ADD). Even if you were diagnosed with the disorder when you were younger and had adjusted well, things may suddenly have become harder. You may feel unbalanced, unfocused, and more frequently overwhelmed. That's all normal. In this book we hope to get you back on the right track again so that you feel more in control and successful.

If you have recently been diagnosed as having ADD, you may have questions about why you are just now finding out about this disorder. You may have been able to cope quite well in elementary school, in a single, self-contained classroom with one primary teacher. However, as you progressed in school and the program demanded more reading and more organizational skills, you may have found it difficult to achieve at the levels you previously attained.

Whether you are just finding out about ADD or have known about the diagnosis for some time, you probably have many questions at this time. What is ADD? How does it manifest in kids my age? What changes will I find in middle school or high school? What areas might I find particularly difficult? How can I do better? All of these questions will be answered in this book. First, let's start by talking about what ADD is and is not.

Attention Deficit Disorder is a neurobiochemical condition resulting from a malfunction in the transmitter systems of the brain. At this time, researchers believe that this system utilizes the neurotransmitter, dopamine, but other transmitters may be involved as well. ADD is *not* the result of brain damage or retardation. Studies of people with ADD have shown that the areas of the brain that are responsible for attention and inhibition are not working as well as they should.

Dr. Alan Zametkin and his colleagues at the National Institutes of Mental Health in Bethesda, Maryland have used special scanners and performed positron emission testing (PET) to measure the metabolic activity of the brain. In these studies they found that certain areas of the brain had diminished activity levels. These results confirmed that certain functions, such as attention and inhibition, that were supposed to be going on in these areas were diminished for biological reasons. While the initial studies were done with adults, subsequent studies have been performed with both adolescent boys and girls, with similar results.

This decrease in functioning in certain areas of the brain is the reason individuals with ADD have trouble paying attention and may daydream or be distracted.

Many factors are involved in the process of paying attention. Initiating, shifting, and sustaining attention, and the ability to develop a plan of action, are considered to be "executive functions" of the brain, or, more specifically, of the frontal lobes of the cerebral cortex. Difficulty in these areas is called an "executive function disorder." Individuals with ADD often have an executive function disorder. They have problems organizing their lives and managing their time. They have difficulty completing projects. They can be forgetful and misplace or lose things.

Some people with ADD are also impulsive. They frequently act or speak without thinking. This causes them to get into trouble or to be accident prone. They may be easily frustrated or get angry quickly. Frequent mood swings, although seen in all adolescents, are more common if you have ADD. You may be happy one minute and feeling "down" or "sad" the next.

Cognitive fatigue is also common in adolescents with ADD. You may tire easily or tend to lack the persistence for completing tasks. Sleep disorders can be present and may include difficulty falling asleep at night and/or waking in the morning. You may feel tired during the day, and you may yawn when concentration is required for a task. Some students have described feeling that they will fall asleep if they sit too long. These problems with arousal contribute to both inattention in class and incompletion of assignments, resulting in underachievement and dissatisfaction with performance by students, parents, and teachers.

While some people with ADD may be physically hyperactive or restless, not all individuals have this aspect of the disorder. In this book, we refer to the syndrome as ADD—Attention Deficit Disorder—and not ADHD—Attention Deficit Hyperactivity Disorder. It seems that by adolescence even those who were hyperactive when younger are less so now. However, they may be fidgety or restless instead. If you are being diagnosed with ADD for the first time when you are older, it is likely that you are not hyperactive. Hyperactivity is usually hard to miss, so the child who is hyperactive is noticed early on.

ADD usually begins before seven years of age but most likely is present from birth. Most kids are diagnosed as having ADD by kindergarten or first grade, particularly if they are hyperactive. The term Attention Deficit Disorder (ADD) describes a syndrome, or set of symptoms, which includes the problems that people with the disorder have to deal with in their daily lives. Having the disorder does not affect intelligence or the way you look, but it does affect the way that you act or feel.

How do you know if you have ADD? The diagnosis can only be made by a professional. It usually involves interviewing you and your parents and determining if you have any of the symptoms described above. Your teachers may be asked to fill out questionnaires to document how you are functioning both academically and behaviorally in the classroom. In addition, you will be referred for psychoeducational testing to establish how your attention problems are affecting your learning and to diagnose any specific learning disabilities. Mental health professionals use a set of criteria to assist in establishing diagnoses. The following are the set of diagnostic criteria used to establish the diagnosis of AD/HD as listed in the American Psychiatric Association's 1994 *Diagnostic and Statistical Manual of Mental Disorders* (DSM-IV).

DIAGNOSTIC CRITERIA FOR ATTENTION DEFICIT/HYPERACTIVITY DISORDER*

Inattention: six or more of the following symptoms that have persisted for at least six months
(a) often fails to give close attention to details or makes careless mistakes in schoolwork, work, or other activities
(b) often has difficulty sustaining attention in tasks or play activities
(c) often does not seem to listen when spoken to directly
(d) often does not follow through on instructions and fails to finish schoolwork, chores, or du-

---

*Reprinted with permission from the *Diagnostic and Statistical Manual of Mental Disorders*, 4th edition. Copyright © 1994 by the American Psychiatric Association.

ties in the workplace (not due to oppositional behavior or failure to understand instructions)

(e) often has difficulties organizing tasks and activities

(f) often avoids, dislikes, or is reluctant to engage in tasks that require sustained mental effort (such as schoolwork or homework)

(g) often loses things necessary for tasks or activities (e.g., toys, school assignments, pencils, books, or tools)

(h) is often distracted by extraneous stimuli

(i) is often forgetful in daily activities

Hyperactivity-impulsivity: six (or more) of the following symptoms have persisted for at least six months

Hyperactivity

(a) often fidgets with hands or feet or squirms in seat

(b) often leaves seat in classroom or in other situations in which remaining seated is expected

(c) often runs about or climbs excessively in situations in which it is inappropriate (in adolescents or adults, may be limited to subjective feelings of restlessness)

(d) often has difficulty playing or engaging in leisure activities quietly

(e) is often "on the go" or often acts as if "driven by a motor"

(f) often talks excessively

Impulsivity

(g) often blurts out answers before questions have been completed

(h) often has difficulty awaiting turn

(i) often interrupts or intrudes on others (e.g., butts into conversations or games)

Even if the diagnosis of ADD is first being made in adolescence, some of the above symptoms that are causing you problems must have been present before the age of seven years and must occur in two or more settings (such as at home and at school) to confirm the diagnosis. These symptoms also must not be caused by another disorder and must significantly impair functioning in social, academic, or work areas.

The disorder is now characterized as having a predominantly inattentive type or a predominantly hyperactive/impulsive type. These types are determined by the characteristics you exhibit. Someone can have both types, which is then referred to as having the combined type of the disorder. Most children and adolescents with ADD have the combined type.

ADD is not determined by a blood test or the examination of your brain waves by an electroencephalogram (EEG) or of your brain structures by CAT or MRI scans. The PET testing that we talked about earlier is useful but is not yet available for determining the diagnosis. At this time, it is only available in the laboratory for scientific studies.

Attention Deficit Disorder may be inherited. Therefore, you may find that there are others in your family with the same or a similar diagnosis. This can sometimes add to your problems as you try to cope with a hyperactive brother or sister. But it can also contribute to your parents' having a better understanding of what you are going through, particularly if your sibling was diagnosed earlier and your parents are accustomed to the symptoms and treatment of ADD. Your parents may also have ADD themselves. They will be more tuned in to your difficulties if they faced similar problems growing up because of their ADD.

As many as 10% of the population may have some form of attention problems, so you are not alone in your classrooms either. You can probably name several other students who are disorganized and have trouble paying attention. Some may have already been diagnosed and take medication to effectively deal with their disorder.

2.◆
AFTER THE DIAGNOSIS, THEN WHAT?

What can be done to make things easier now that you have been diagnosed with ADD? The answer to that question involves a combination of many things. An effective treatment program that addresses all aspects of your ADD may include medication, counseling, tutoring, accommodations in the classroom, and adaptation of your academic program.

MEDICATION

One of the most effective treatments for attentional deficits is medication. Ninety percent of individuals diagnosed with ADD who take medication are given stimulants. These include Ritalin, Dexedrine, and Cylert. We do not know exactly how the stimulants work, but most likely they are involved in enhancing the effectiveness of the neurotransmitters that we discussed in the first chapter. They are thought to improve transmissions in those areas of the brain that are responsible for inhibiting and for performing executive functions. The chart below lists the various stimulants and other medications and their common dosage forms.

MEDICATIONS CURRENTLY USED IN THE TREATMENT OF AD/HD IN ADOLESCENTS

Name	Dose available (Range)	Onset / Duration
Stimulants		
Methylphenidate		
Ritalin	5, 10, 20 mg tablets (5–80 mg/day)	20 minutes/ lasts 3–5 hours
Ritalin SR	20 mg sustained release (20–80 mg/day)	45–60 minutes/ lasts 6–8 hours
Dextroamphetamine		
Dexedrine	5 mg tablets (2.5–40 mg/day)	20–30 minutes/ lasts 3–5 hours
Dexedrine Spansules	5, 10, 15 mg capsules (5–40 mg/day)	60 minutes/lasts 6–10 hours
Pemoline		
Cylert	18.75, 37.5, 75 mg (18.75–112.5 mg/ day)	12–24 hours[*]
Nonstimulants		
Clonidine		
Catapres	0.1, 0.2, 0.3 mg tablets (0.1–0.3 mg/day)	8–12 hours[*]

Catapres TTS	1, 2, 3 patches (0.1–0.3 mg/day)	lasts 5–7 days[*]

Antidepressants

Imipramine Tofranil	10, 25, 50 mg tablets (25–200 mg/day)	12–24 hours[*]
Desipramine Norpramin	10, 25, 50, 75 mg tablets (25–200 mg/day)	12–24 hours[*]
Fluoxetine Prozac	10, 20 mg pulvules Liquid 20 mg/5 ml (10–60 mg/day)	2–4 weeks half-life of several days
Sertraline Zoloft	50, 100 mg tablets (50–200 mg/day)	2–3 weeks half-life 24 hours
Paroxetine Paxil	20, 30 mg tablets (10–40 mg/day)	2–3 weeks half-life 14 hours

[*]Takes several weeks to reach effective levels

While stimulants are effective, they do have some side effects. These include appetite suppression, trouble sleeping, jitteriness, headaches, and stomachaches. Pemoline, or Cylert, can cause liver dysfunction. If you are taking this drug it is important to have routine blood tests about every three months to monitor the status of your liver functions.

Stimulants also interact negatively with drugs and alcohol. The combination of stimulants and cocaine can be lethal. The majority of adolescents realize that drugs and alcohol mess up your brain and life, areas that adolescents with ADD are working very hard to make better.

Other medications are also used, either alone or in combination with the stimulants, to treat related symptoms. These include clonidine and antidepressants. Clonidine works on the systems that control symptoms of overarousal. It addresses both sleep disorders and overanxiety and is used for aggressive behaviors. Clonidine also is used to treat tics and obsessive-compulsive behaviors.

Commonly used antidepressants include Prozac, Zoloft, Tofranil, and Norpramin. These may be used in combination with stimulants to address symptoms of depression or obsessive-compulsive behaviors. Some cases of ADD are more severe or complicated, and these tend to respond better to combinations of medication than to stimulants alone. Prozac and Zoloft are also quite effective in treating panic disorders when these are present along with ADD. Side effects of most antidepressants include drowsiness and gastrointestinal problems.

When taking one of the tricyclic antidepressants (such as imipramine or desipramine), it is important to monitor blood levels to make sure these levels stay within the therapeutic range. An EKG to monitor cardiac status should also be obtained prior to treatment and following any significant increase in dose.

Common side effects to medications used to treat AD/HD and strategies to manage them are listed in the chart on the next page. While this chart presents sug-

SIDE EFFECTS OF MEDICATIONS

Side Effect	*Management Strategy**
Stimulants	
Appetite decrease/nausea	Eat several small meals a day Take medication after meals with a full glass of juice or water Increase regular exercise
Stomachaches/headaches	Usually relieved by eating; don't skip meals
Weight loss	Increase calories or add supplements
Insomnia	Contact your physician for a possible decrease in dose late in the day or add clonidine at bedtime Increase regular exercise
Irritability	Decrease caffeine intake Contact your physician for a change to Dexedrine or overlap doses if increases when medicine wears off
Tics	Contact your physician to decrease dose, add clonidine, or change medication
Depressed mood Social withdrawal	Contact your physician for reevaluation of medication
Antidepressants	
Sedation/fatigue	Will gradually decrease over time Begin by taking medicine at bedtime
Dry mouth/dizziness	Drink plenty of liquids
Gastrointestinal distress	Take after meals Increase fiber
Nervousness/tremor/anxiety	Contact your physician to decrease dose or change medication

Sudden increase in hyperactive or manic behaviors	Contact your physician
Insomnia	Contact your physican to decrease dose or change medication
Rash	Contact your physician

*Always contact your physician before making any changes in your medication or to report serious side effects.

gestions to decrease side effects, it is not a substitute for medical advice. If you have any concerns or serious side effects while taking medication, it is always important to contact your doctor immediately. You should never decrease your prescribed dose of medicine or discontinue treatment without discussing it with a physician.

If your physician has prescribed medication for you, make sure you take an active part in the treatment process. This includes having regular discussions regarding effectiveness and any possible side effects. Make sure that you feel comfortable with taking the medicine as prescribed and that you have had all your questions answered.

Some students with ADD feel uncomfortable about taking the medicine at school. Long-acting forms of the drugs are available and may address this issue. Within the school setting, the school nurse is also available to assist you.

3.◆

HELP IS ONLY A
SCHOOL NURSE AWAY

by Peggie Ravida, R.N., B.S.N

If you are diagnosed with ADD, whether you take medication or not, the school nurse can help you learn more about your diagnosis and how to live successfully with it. She is a professional trained in medicine and is used to talking to kids about all sorts of problems. If you do take medication to address symptoms of your ADD, the nurse is someone you should definitely get to know. The idea of taking medication at school may seem scary at first, but with a little help and reassurance you'll soon be an old hand at it.

Preplanning Can Make Taking Medication Easy

◆ Check on the specific medication policy at your school.

◆ Doctor's orders should state your name, your diagnosis, the name of the medication, the dosage or amount, and the time to be given.

◆ A separate prescription bottle, correctly labeled, should be brought into school by your parent.

◆ Your parents will probably have to sign a form giving their consent for the medication to be given at school.

◆ Establish the best time to take your medication at school. It could be right before lunch or between classes. The time depends on what medication you are taking, how long it lasts, and what time you take it in the morning.

Tricks of the Trade

Some things are hard to remember until they become a habit. Until taking your medication becomes a habit, you'll have to devise ways to remind yourself to take it on time.

- ◆ Place a note in your lunch or desk or book.
- ◆ Set your watch to go off at the right time.
- ◆ Find a buddy, another student who goes to get his or her medication at the same time.
- ◆ Be creative, make your own secret code.

Taking the Pill

- ◆ Always tell the person who is administering your medication your full name so no mistakes will be made.
- ◆ If possible look at the bottle they are pouring it from to make sure that it is yours.
- ◆ Check that you have been given the correct number of tablets.
- ◆ Take your medication with a glass of water. Now is a good time to get in one of those eight glasses of water you should be drinking daily.

You should report any side effects such as headaches, stomachaches, difficulty sleeping, or feeling jittery. However, these side effects usually go away in a few days. Taking your medicine after you eat, instead of before, may help. Hopefully, you will be able to get more work done and not miss important information in class. Sometimes you won't see the difference, but your teachers and parents will.

Dosage, or How Much Will I Take?

Doctors usually calculate the correct dosage for medicine based on your body weight. However, they probably will start you on the smallest amount and gradually increase the dosage until your teachers and parents see that you are more attentive. As you get older and grow bigger, the dosage may be increased.

Your Work Is Not Over

Medication is not the *only* answer. The pills are not "magic." You need to do your part and become better informed. Some school nurses hold groups for students who have AD/HD. It's helpful to know that you are not alone. Talking to other students eases stress and gives you ideas on how they manage to succeed in class. If you don't have a group, start one at your school or find one in your community.

Spreading the News

There are other things that can be done to help you at school. With your parents' permission, the school nurse can inform your teachers about your diagnosis and make sure they understand how to help you in the classroom. The nurse can also observe in the classroom to make suggestions to the teachers about the class structure and routine and how it affects you. The teacher can help by assigning you a seat up front, adjusting assignments, repeating directions, and giving you a secret sign when you are off task. Be sure to read the chapter on accommodations to explain these and other suggestions that might be useful for you.

Don't Forget

You have an ally in the school nurse. She is there to help you in any way that she can. Go talk to her even if you are not taking medication and make a new friend who will always be willing to listen to your side of every story.

4.◆

IS HAVING ADD A LIFE SENTENCE?

Although the picture of ADD can change as you grow and mature, attentional deficits remain in 60% of individuals diagnosed with ADD. While some symptoms (such as hyperactivity) may lessen, others (such as difficulty concentrating and organizing) can remain through adulthood. You, however, do not need to think of your attentional problems as a life sentence. There are things that you can do to affect the impact of ADD on your life. This book will present some ideas and plans of actions that you might consider.

First, always remember that there are lots of good aspects to having ADD. Don't always dwell on the negative. For starters, you are usually as smart or smarter than others in your class, as ADD does not affect intelligence. Second, individuals with ADD can be very creative and artistically talented. They have lots of great ideas; they just need help in following through and bringing them to completion. Third, people with ADD have lots of energy and are always on the go. This can be an advantage, particularly if you like sports and want to take time to develop that talent.

Many teens that I see in my practice are concerned not only about how long the symptoms of ADD will last but also about how long they will need treatment. Will they take medication forever? Will they need tutoring throughout their school career? While the answers to these questions always depend on the individual, there are some general statements that can be made.

There is no "cure" for ADD, and the symptoms, while they change over time, do not always go away completely. In one of the classic follow-up studies of children initially diagnosed with ADD between the ages of 6 and 13 years, all reported restlessness as the main problem. Five years later, restlessness was no longer the primary complaint for any one of them. Thirty percent of the group reported that restlessness was still present but not a severe problem. Distractibility and poor concentration were now the chief complaints in 46% of the study subjects. Problems with peer relationships were reported in 30%, and problems with academic achievement were seen in 80% of the group.

Because of these problems with academic achievement, tutoring or accommodations are usually necessary to help adolescents with ADD achieve success in school. Tutoring can be undertaken to improve organizational skills or to address weak content areas. In my practice I find that students who are just being diagnosed in high school may have missed some basic concepts or information along the way when they were not paying attention. It is important to remediate these areas as soon as possible and to address any organizational weaknesses.

Medication may be necessary to improve focus and concentration both in class and when you are studying or doing homework. However, I find that no student takes medication forever. As you get older you will decide, along with your doctor, when it is appropriate that you take your medication and when you no longer need it for certain tasks.

Regardless of what you decide to do now, remember that having ADD does not have to be a life sentence. Think of it rather as a certain lifestyle that you need to adopt to be successful.

In addition to their ADD, it is not uncommon for adolescents to be diagnosed with other disorders that commonly go along with ADD. Up to 40% of individuals with ADD also have another diagnosis. These conditions include depression, tics (involuntary repetitive motor movements), Tourette Syndrome (a neurobiochemical disorder that involves attentional deficits and tics), obsessive-compulsive disorder, anxiety disorder, and learning disabilities. These disorders need to be diagnosed and treated in addition to your ADD symptoms if you are to successfully deal with all aspects of your life.

Remember, if you are feeling depressed, sad, or hopeless, it is important to seek treatment for these symptoms, too. Some students with ADD become depressed because things are not going as well as they would like. Other teens may have a primary depressive disorder for which they need treatment.

Adolescence is a period of rapid growth and development. Hormonal changes are taking place in your body, and you may find that you have an increasing need for sleep or that you are now always hungry. Getting plenty of rest is important for proper growth and development. Some teens with ADD may have difficulty falling asleep or may be sleepy all the time, even falling asleep in class. You need to discuss this with your physician to determine if an adjustment in medication might help you fall asleep better at night or keep you awake in class.

However, you should be the one to try to establish a schedule or routine for yourself. Starting to study at 10 o'clock at night, staying up to talk on the telephone, or watching the late night shows on TV can create problems in your natural biological rhythms. Sleep deprivation can make you irritable, less able to think clearly, or cause you to doze off in class, thereby missing important material.

Some adolescents attempt to stay awake by loading up on caffeine. Too much caffeine can make you jittery. It is also a stimulant, and, while moderate amounts may help you be more alert, excess amounts can actually interfere with functioning. Excess caffeine also reacts with the stimulant medication you are taking to control your attention problems and can heighten the negative side effects of appetite suppression and insomnia.

Appetite suppression can be a bothersome side effect of taking stimulants, but not all people on stimulants experience this negative effect. If you find you do have a decreased appetite and don't feel like eating most of the time, discuss this with your doctor. Regardless, it is important that you eat nutritious foods regularly. You may find it more difficult to eat large meals when on medication for ADD. Try eating several smaller meals throughout the day. These should consist of protein and complex carbohydrates (breads, pasta, rice, and crackers). Too much sugar in your diet is not good for you either. It can wreak havoc with your insulin response and blood sugar levels.

For the same reasons, it is also important to avoid skipping meals. Research has consistently shown that when a person skips a meal or is fasting he or she makes more errors on testing. In addition, I find that my patients who skip meals tend to get more stomachaches and headaches when taking stimulant medications. Regular meals help avoid these side effects.

Regular exercise is also very important. Many of my patients report that they burn off extra energy by running, jogging, or swimming. This also keeps them fit and helps them to feel better. They insist that they are less hyperactive and that they can sit for longer periods after exercising vigorously.

Through medication, proper exercise, and diet you are trying to achieve proper balance and equilibrium in the biochemical functioning in your brain. It is therefore important that you avoid habits that can upset this balance and "mess up" the equilibrium that you have worked so hard to achieve. Alcohol and drugs can do just that, in addition to endangering your health and well-being.

Unfortunately, today, it has become extremely popular to abuse Ritalin and Dexedrine, as well as other drugs. This not only reflects poor judgment but can be extremely dangerous. Students have died of sudden cardiac arrest after consuming alcohol and "snorting" Ritalin. Taken at the prescribed dosage level, Dexedrine can be extremely effective in addressing the symptoms of ADD. However, when abused it can lead to serious negative effects of extreme weight loss, insomnia, and nervous habits such as picking at your skin. Students who abuse amphetamines can become addicted very quickly. At extremely high dosages, amphetamines can cause hallucinations and paranoid or psychotic reactions.

You need to be in control of yourself and your medications at all times. Establish the ground rules with your friends early. Your medication has been prescribed for you for a specific purpose after careful diagnostic testing. Never "help out" a friend by allowing him or her to try your medication. You are the one responsible for making sure that your medication is not sold or stolen.

5. ◆
OTHER THINGS ARE IMPORTANT, TOO

While ADD is an important part of your life there are many other important aspects to consider as well. ADD should not be your defining characteristic! You have many other qualities and talents to focus on and enjoy.

If you are like other kids with ADD, you have outside interests and activities that keep you busy. If you play sports, you may have practice every day after

school. You are now involved in more social activities
with your friends. Going to concerts, parties, and dances
now takes up some of your free time. You may play a
musical instrument, which requires daily practice. You
may even have a part-time job. Good for you! These are
all great activities. They are not only fun but they are
ways to express yourself and your talents.

SPORTS

You may find that you are well coordinated and ex-
cel in athletics. Many students with ADD have excep-
tional athletic abilities. High school provides ample opportunities for you to develop in this area. Increased
skill and confidence as well as a greater commitment
are necessary to participate in sports at the high school
level. You may find that the time required for practice
has increased dramatically. While previously your coach
held practice twice a week, daily practice may now be
required. Some students find it difficult to allocate time
to both sports and studies. Others report that they do
better when their afternoon schedule is filled and they
are forced to be more organized.

If you want to try a new sport or hone your athletic
ability, by all means sign up and try it out, but beware
of difficulties. Some students have reported that they
encounter problems during practice because of their
ADD. They have trouble staying focused or get restless
or bored. This may give the coach the impression that

they are not interested or that they give up too quickly. If you encounter these problems but still want to play the sport, do not give up. There are several steps you can take.

First, speak to the coaching staff and let them know that you have ADD and are having some of the symptoms described above. Try to work out some signals or other means by which you can communicate your need for a break. Some individual sessions with a coach may help you master the skills needed or the drills being used. Be sure to express your desire to be part of the team and encourage the coach to not allow you to quit.

Second, if you take medication to improve your ability to concentrate, discuss with your physician the possibility of your taking a dose before participating in practices or games. Many students report that this helps them focus better on the fundamentals, improves their precision, and keeps them from getting distracted by extraneous stimuli. They are better able to execute plays and focus on the playing field.

Third, if team sports turn out not to be your forte, try one of the sports where you compete as an individual. Track, golf, tennis, and swimming are good examples.

Karate also offers teens with ADD an excellent opportunity to enhance self-esteem, improve skills, and gain control. It helps in establishing the mind's control over the body. Combined with meditation it can be very effective in dealing with the symptoms of ADD and can also be quite relaxing.

◆ ◆ ◆

My name is Keith Crim. I am 15 years old and have a second degree black belt in Shorin-Rye karate. I also have a second degree black-belt in weapons. I enjoy karate a lot and have been working at it since I was seven years old. I have won over 18 trophies and some 30 medals and participated in many tournaments. I have been both state and national champion.

Karate is excellent for people who have ADD or ADHD. I have ADHD, and karate has helped me in many ways. It has taught me self-discipline and control. It is not an easy sport, but it gets you in shape in both mind and body. You have to be motivated to learn what you need to know in order to test for your next belt. It felt good as I moved through the belt ranks to have the younger students look up to me. It's great to see how far I have gotten in karate, at this time I am the highest ranking teenager in my dojo. I already know a lot about karate, but one thing that it has taught me is that I still have a lot to learn and that you can never know everything.

◆ ◆ ◆

Many of my patients tell me that they need to exercise regularly. If you are not involved in any organized sport, take up something like jogging, in-line skating, bicycling, or aerobics. The exercise you get will both keep you in shape and help you control your feelings of restlessness.

FRIENDSHIPS, DATING, AND SOCIAL SKILLS

Many kids with ADD have no difficulty making and keeping friends. That is because they are charming, good looking, empathetic, friendly, and have a good sense of humor. However, some kids with ADD feel that they need to adopt the role of "class clown" in order to be well liked and to gain attention for themselves. While this is one coping mechanism for dealing with some of the symptoms of ADD, it is not always the most effective. Teachers easily become annoyed, and your friends don't take you seriously. They feel that you are always just "clowning around."

While there are many positive aspects to the personality of someone with ADD, there are also some characteristics of ADD that interfere with friendships and social relationships. Impulsivity (acting without thinking) may cause you to change your mind or your plans frequently. This may drive your friends crazy. It can also lead you to blurt out statements without thinking about how they will affect others or reflect upon yourself. People with ADD often tend to interrupt others while they are speaking or to monopolize the conversation with their own agenda. Sometimes you may be thinking of something completely different while others are talking and then make a comment that is irrelevant to the conversation. Your friends may respond, "What are you talking about?" Then everyone is confused.

ADD can interfere with paying attention to the body language of others or to those subtle cues in the environment that give you feedback on how to react or re-

spond in a given situation. Temper outbursts and mood swings may also cause difficulty in your relationships both at home and at school. It is difficult for others to relate to someone whose mood is always changing. Since they don't know how you are going to react, people may avoid you or act nervous or quiet around you.

As a teen, you are now beginning to date. Each person seems to have a different approach to dating. If you are shy, you may have difficulty meeting people or asking them out. Joining a club or seeking activities that you have in common may help you meet other teens. Some teens prefer to "date" or go out with a group of friends. There is no established "right" time to begin dating. Do what feels comfortable to you, when you are ready.

Talk things over with your parents and keep them informed about your friends and activities. They enjoy hearing about them and have had some of the same feelings and experiences themselves.

Sometimes teens with ADD behave impulsively when it comes to dating. They shift partners or break dates without thinking through their decisions or realizing the consequences involved. There have been many "broken hearts" as a teen with ADD impulsively changed dates right before the prom. Just remember, as in all other areas, you are responsible for your actions and having ADD is not an excuse for inappropriate behavior. Anyone can show that they care for another person by being considerate and thoughtful.

Symptoms of ADD may lead to difficulty maintaining friendships or a dating relationship, but it is important that you not give up and keep working on these problems. A good friend will understand and be willing to help you through the difficult times. If you are honest and open about specific behaviors that seem to bother you or others, you and your friends can work out ways to solve these problems together.

DRIVING

If you are like every other teen, you can't wait until you are old enough to get your driver's license. The license symbolizes your independence and opens new avenues to work and recreation. But passing the test and getting that license may not be as easy as you imag-

ined. Driving a car is a very complex activity. It involves processing many stimuli and actions simultaneously. Some teens with ADD have difficulty handling so many stimuli at one time. It will require a lot of practice and perseverance to accomplish this goal, but you can do it, just as you have conquered other difficult tasks.

Distractibility and lack of impulse control may also cause problems once you are driving. Studies have shown that adolescents with ADD are involved in more accidents because their attention problems interfere with concentration while driving. Looking at something that attracts your attention on the side of the road may cause you to miss noticing that the traffic ahead has come to a stop, leading to an accident. Teens with ADHD also tend to get more speeding tickets because they are either not in control or distracted. Impulsivity behind the wheel can have serious consequences.

Lack of attention to small details, such as the gas gauge, has also been known to cause some teens with ADD to take many an unexpected walk as they ran out of gas without a station in sight for miles. This turn of events can make you late for your planned activity or curfew and cause additional difficulties with friends and parents.

One way to be better prepared is to take driver's education classes. I also recommend that my patients drive with another adult for period of time to reinforce skills even after they actually do get their license. If medication helps you be less impulsive and distractible, you should also discuss taking your medication before driving.

It is important for you to seriously evaluate your own abilities. If you can't drive well, don't drive. This is a critical decision and one that requires a lot of maturity. If you can't concentrate, your friends would rather drive you than drive with you. Ask for their help. Explain your problem and they will understand. No one should drive after drinking alcohol or doing drugs, and no one should drive if they feel distracted. Leave the driving to others, prevent accidents, and save lives.

6.◆

LET'S GET ORGANIZED

Now that you are so busy, with so many demands on your time, you need to organize all your activities and your school assignments. Remember, no matter how important and fun all these other activities are, you are still a STUDENT.

SCHEDULING

One way to help you become better organized is to create a schedule, but how to get started? First, start by creating a daily schedule like the one below. This shows you everything that you have to do each day after school.

Sample After-School Schedule
Monday, December 7th

3:00 Return books to library; meet with math teacher to discuss test
4:00 Basketball practice
6:00 Home
6:30 Shower and dinner
7:30 Talk on phone with friends

8:00   Homework
9:00   Break for snack
9:15   Homework
10:00   Review for math test; write schedule for tomorrow
11:00   Pack book bag; remember to bring gym shoes and permission for field trip
11:15   Prepare for bed
11:30   Bed

Next let's look at a plan for a week. Keeping a calendar like this for each week or month helps you to organize your time and PLAN AHEAD for big projects. This is a good way to look at the "big picture" and avoid leaving everything to the one night you also have a big basketball game or have to study for a test in addition to your other homework.

Sample Weekly Calendar

DECEMBER

7 Mon	*English term paper due* *Basketball practice 4-6*
8 Tues	*Math Test* *P E - field trip permission slip due* *Basketball practice 4-6*
9 Wed	*Piano lesson 3-3:30* *Basketball practice 4-6*

10 Thurs	*Vocab Quiz* *Get haircut afterschool* *Basketball practice 4-6*
11 Fri	*Spanish Test - 1st period* *Basketball Game 7:30 gym*

ORGANIZING LONG-TERM ASSIGNMENTS

But how can you keep track of tests and when long-term assignments are due? A large planning calendar can be particularly useful. These can usually be purchased at an office supply store and then tacked up on your wall. When you fill in all your assignments, you will be able to see at a glance all the work you have to do. Be sure to break down your large projects or long-term assignments into manageable pieces.

For a project that is assigned April 18th and due May 16th, for example, try to talk to your teacher and set up a schedule. It might go something like this.

> April 27th—declare topic
> May 2nd—get books from library; do research and compile bibliography
> May 9th—turn in outline
> May 12th—turn in rough draft
> May 16th—turn in final report

Presenting a rough draft to your teacher can help assure success for several reasons. It shows you are working toward completion. It allows the teacher to give you feedback so you can determine if you are on the right track with the project. Deficiencies can be pointed out early. By following your teacher's suggestions, you are more likely to get a better grade. Finally, if necessary, the teacher might give you an extension to incorporate his or her suggestions.

Test grades can also be entered on your planning calendar. Seeing them clearly written out can give you a rough estimate of your progress, need for extra work, and standings before interim or final grades are mailed out.

ORGANIZING YOUR SPACE

It is also important to organize your space at home. Try to find a quiet distraction-free environment in which you feel comfortable to do your homework and studying. Make sure that it is equipped with everything you will need (paper, pens, tape, stapler, compass, etc). Some students feel that quiet music playing in the background helps them focus better. If you are one of these, be sure to discuss this with your parents and present clearly your reasons for wanting to have music while you are studying.

ORGANIZING YOUR HOMEWORK

Here are several suggestions to make homework go more smoothly. Check over the assignment sheet where you have written the work for the day or week. Set priorities for your homework for the evening, using a red pen or marker to number each subject. Don't leave the most difficult work for last, since that is when you will be most tired. Also remember your need for breaks. Schedule those into your study plan as you divide the assignments into manageable sections. Remember that portions of long-term projects and reading assignments need to be scheduled in as part of each night's homework.

MISSING ASSIGNMENTS

Missing assignments appear to be a common cause of lower grades for most students with ADD. Waiting until the end of the marking period to find out assignments are missing is not a good idea. The amount of work is usually overwhelming at that point, and it is too late to get the missing assignments all done. A weekly assignment checksheet can help address this problem in a timely and manageable fashion. This sheet has several advantages. It enables you to discover weekly what assignments are missing. Keeping up with assignments allows for better follow-up and understanding of material being presented. Quiz and test performance usually improves when you are prepared on a daily and weekly basis. Knowing that the assignments will have to be completed each weekend motivates many students to finish them when assigned during the week.

On the next page is a sample of an assignment checksheet. Discuss such a sheet with your parents and advisor at school.

WEEKLY ASSIGNMENT CHECKSHEET

Name: _____ **Date:** _____

SUBJECT	TEACHER INITIALS	MISSING ASSIGNMENTS

To be initialed each week by all teachers.

Consequences

1. If student forgets sheet—Grounded for weekend.
2. Missing assignments must be completed before any contact with friends, TV, phone, etc., Friday p.m. or Saturday a.m. **No exceptions** (even for a sports activity).
3. If all signed as clear and completed—Prearranged **reward** for weekend (pizza, sleepover, movie, later curfew, etc.).

7.◆
TIPS FOR SCHOOL SUCCESS

Underachievement in school is the primary concern of most students with ADD. They find it difficult to get all the work done. It seems to take them two or three times as long to complete work that other students do in a much shorter time and with less effort. Missing assignments and low test grades appear to be major contributors to overall poor performance. Students are generally dissatisfied with their poor grades, especially after they put in so much time and effort, but they don't know what to do about them.

Don't despair. Success can be yours. There are ways to address these problems, and in this chapter we will share some of them with you. However, it is up to you to make use of these tips and gain back the advantage in school. Remember, hard work does pay off! Students with ADD need to work harder than other students, and they need to work more efficiently. You also need to be aware of what accommodations work for you.

ACCOMMODATIONS THAT WORK

Computers/Word Processors/Calculators

Many students with ADD have difficulty with written assignments. They have poor handwriting or difficulty with organization or proofreading skills. Using a computer or word processor can help with these difficulties. The computer allows for editing and better organization of thoughts and ideas. It seems that students with ADD are better able to compose and organize material on the computer. A spell check and thesaurus can be invaluable if poor spelling or word retrieval difficulties impair your writing ability. A laptop computer may also assist in and improve class notetaking skills. Using a calculator can help eliminate careless math mistakes, which so frequently plague the student with attention difficulties and lead to the lowering of grades on tests and quizzes.

Untimed Tests

As a result of problems with timely recall, poor time management, perceptual difficulties, disorganization, and difficulty writing, many students with ADD need to make arrangements to take untimed tests or be given extended time for testing. This accommodation may be needed for classroom tests as well as for standardized testing, including the PSATs and SATs. Only students whose school currently provides them with special ac-

commodations for instruction and assessment are eligible for extended time or other special arrangements on the SAT, however.

What You Need for Permission to Take the SATs Untimed

The current Educational Testing Service (ETS) requirements for eligibility to take untimed SATs are as follows: A student must have on file at his or her school either a current Individual Education Program (IEP) or two signed documents, based on test results obtained during the previous three years from any of the following: physicians, psychologists, child study teams, or LD specialists. Both documents cannot be from the same individual or team.

When a public school normally provides an IEP for the student with a learning disability, that student may not present signed statements in lieu of an IEP in order to obtain extended time and/or other special test arrangements. The IEP must state the nature and effect of the disability and the need for modified testing arrangements. In addition, the signed documents must affirm that the disability meets state guidelines for certification when such guidelines exist. The IEP or two signed documents are then retained in the school file unless specifically requested by the SAT Services for Students with Disabilities.

Tape Recorders and Books on Tape

Some students find using a tape recorder in class helpful. It allows them to relisten to the material and fill in and verify information in their notes. It is particularly useful to tape the class before a test, when the teacher is reviewing the material that will be covered on the test. Students who are auditory learners find that Books on Tape help them to process information more easily. For students with a reading disability, these tapes can allow better access to material. You can apply for books on tape at your local public library. It is a service provided for all persons with reading disabilities. You can also write to the National Library Service for the Blind and Physically Handicapped, Library of Congress, Washington, DC 20542 for an application form and the addresses of cooperating libraries.

Recordings for the Blind is a private organization that lends free recorded textbooks and other educational materials to the blind and visually handicapped people or those with specific learning disabilities. There is a small registration fee. Detailed information about this service and an application can be obtained from: Recording for the Blind, Inc., 20 Rozel Road, Princeton, NJ 08540.

Notetakers and Class Notes

Students who have difficulty taking complete notes in class may want to arrange to obtain a copy of class notes or to use other students as notetakers. Sometimes arrangements can be made with teachers ahead of time to provide copies of their class notes. An alternative plan is to arrange for another student to take notes on special carbon paper. This is preferable to taking the notes of other students for copying, since the notetakers then wouldn't have access to their own notes for studying.

Preferential Seating

Where you sit in class is important. You need to be away from distractions such as windows and doors that open into hallways. And, yes, distractions include your friends. If you are inclined to talk to them instead of paying attention, changing your seat could really improve your attention and school work.

Advisors and School Counselors

Students with ADD at the high school level continue to need an advisor or school counselor to ensure that their programs are running smoothly. You should meet with the advisor on a weekly, if not a daily, basis to discuss day-to-day functioning and to monitor your academic progress. This advisor can also assist in setting up a schedule that meets your individual needs. Having academic subjects earlier in the day or an additional study hall to organize your daily work can be invaluable for assuring success.

MORE HELPFUL TIPS

Other common problems for students with ADD are reading comprehension, proofreading written assignments, taking notes, and math skills. This section presents ways to improve these skills. It also gives some suggestions for how to study more effectively for tests. Most of these suggestions have been provided by Judith Stern, M.A., an educational consultant from Rockville, Maryland, who uses them in her practice.

Improving Reading Comprehension

Before you begin your actual reading assignment, skim over the chapter of the novel or textbook to familiarize yourself with the material being covered. Look at all the pictures and graphs and read the headings and bold print. Take note of any words that are unfamiliar to you. Look them up or ask a parent or tutor to help you understand their meanings. By doing this ahead of time, once you begin reading you will have a better understanding of passages that would previously have been unclear.

Our comprehension is usually better when we define a purpose for reading before we start. Are you reading a short story to find examples of exaggeration? A chapter in your history textbook to find the most important causes of the Civil War? You will find that you read with a different pace and intensity depending on what you are looking for.

Some students find that they comprehend better if they underline or make notes in the margin or on another piece of paper as they go along. It is also a good idea to read the questions you are supposed to answer *before* you read the chapter. Keep a pencil and paper nearby so you can write answers as you read.

If you find that you lose your place or are sometimes just reading the WORDS and not paying attention to their MEANING, it may help to underline or highlight key ideas, to place a ruler or marker under each line, or to look up frequently from the page to prevent you from just automatically looking at the words and turning the pages.

Try reading the chapter a second time. You will catch many things you did not notice the first time you read. Also be sure to read while you are fresh and not tired out and ready for bed or sleep. Don't leave reading for last. It is an important part of your assignments. If you take medication to help you concentrate, make sure that it is still effective when you attempt your reading assignments. Taking an additional dose of medication before reading may improve attention and comprehension.

Improving Proofreading

When finishing an assignment, read what you have just written out loud. Does it make sense? Did you leave words out or add unnecessary words? Try proofreading with a partner. Sometimes it is easier to spot errors when it is not your own work. If your handwriting is difficult to read, type your rough draft so it is easier to see your errors. Proofread your work first for spelling errors or use a spellcheck. Then go back and check the paper for correct grammar and punctuation. Proofreading from the bottom of the page up also helps you spot spelling errors you might have missed otherwise.

Improving Notetaking

Skip lines when you take notes. This will make it easier to read back what you have written and to add new ideas. Use abbreviations that you will later recognize. Keep a "key" of your own abbreviations in the front of your notebook as a reference. Leave out unimportant words (the, an) that take extra time to write. Keep a few pens and use the ones that you particularly like; that makes writing feel less of an effort. Listen when your teacher uses words that signal something important is about to be said. Here are some examples: "You need to remember..." "There are three important reasons for..." Such phrases let you know that important information will follow.

When definitions are dictated, you might ask the teacher for a copy of the material beforehand. If this is not available and you are slow at notetaking, learn to leave spaces or gaps in your notes, which you can fill in later with the correct information. If you use this technique, you will avoid getting too far behind and missing more of the material.

Improving Math Scores

With math, it is important to be aware when you start to feel lost in a specific unit. Let your teacher or tutor know immediately. Since math is taught as a sequence of concepts, it is important to keep up. Consider practicing math (worksheets, review book, summer school, tutoring) during the summer, since it is easy to forget material learned the previous semester.

When you write up your math examples, pay attention to lining up your numbers in columns. Leave space between examples, so that there is plenty of room to spread out your work. If your teacher gives out math dittos with crowded examples, consider transferring your work to a separate sheet or enlarging the ditto on a copy machine. Make it a habit to check over each math solution on a test before handing it in. Put a small check mark next to each problem after you have checked it.

Improving Studying for Tests

A variety of techniques can help you prepare for tests. Studying with a partner may help you concentrate or improve your understanding of the material. Study cards allow you to review the material both when you make them and every time you go over them. You can also record information into a tape recorder and listen to it over and over. Write or type up your own review sheet of the important concepts that you have learned. Use the main headings and subheadings in your text-book to develop a study outline for yourself. Divide your lecture notes and homework sheets into topics or small manageable sections. Study a portion of these each night. Save the last two nights to review everything, after the material has become more familiar. Plan to spread out your studying. Figure out how long you will need to review all of the material, then add on another two days. If your teacher normally provides you with a review sheet, ask if you might have yours a few days earlier. If the teacher doesn't usually give one, ask if he or she would work one out for you to use.

By leaving plenty of time to study for the test, you should be able to avoid last minute cramming. Getting plenty of sleep the night before a test is also essential. A final bit of advice. Relax! If you find that before or during a test you are becoming anxious, STOP. Take a few depth breaths, and clear your mind. Think of some-thing that you know or write down a few facts related to the test materials you studied. This may help trig-ger an answer and make you feel more confident in your abilities.

8.◆
KIDS TALK ABOUT ADD

The students in this chapter would like to tell you their stories in their own words. They have all been diagnosed with ADD and have had to answer many questions and deal with many of the same problems that you have had. Although these kids all go to different schools, you will see that their experiences are similar to yours. Whether you attend a large public high school or a small private academy, the symptoms of ADD consistently interfere with attention span and organizational skills. When you have ADD, getting your work done is a problem no matter what grade you are in or how smart you are. Let's hear what these students have to say!

◆ NATALIE ◆

It is Monday morning, and my alarm wakes me at 4:30 a.m. I have to finish my history paper. Somehow the weekend got away from me. I tiptoe downstairs to the computer, so I won't wake my parents, who would kill me if they knew I had not finished my work. Half asleep, I turn on the computer, and all of the words are a blur. I can't wing it like I used to. Now I have a bigger problem. As I dash upstairs, I hear my carpool's horn outside, and I search hopelessly through piles of clothes and books for my uniform skirt and shoes. By now, my mother is screaming, "Hurry up! You're going to make everyone late again!" I grab the wrinkled skirt, settle on my sneakers (improper shoes means another demerit), and dart out the door. Halfway to school, I realize my history paper is still on the desk downstairs.

Attending an academically challenging private school did not work to my advantage. I stood out. Most of my peers were focused; therefore, they did not have the behavioral problems I did. Because I had difficulty focusing on the material taught in class, I tried to chat with my peers as a substitute for listening. Teachers corrected me at least three or four times a day. I never realized the consequences until the interim reports citing inattention in class, missed homework, and low tests scores arrived. I knew I had the ability, I never knew what missing work would do to my average. A hard-earned B+ on the *Hamlet* paper could not make up for an F on the unfinished *Othello* paper buried somewhere under my desk.

Because I was generally smart enough, for years I could compensate for my ADD, until things fell apart my sophomore year. In addition to my academic load, I was playing three sports. I never quite could fulfill my potential in the area of athletics. Coaches like to see players who are disciplined and focused. One needs to be disciplined and organized to handle a schedule like that. Even after being tested and diagnosed with ADD (on one attentional test, I scored on the third grade level!), the success story you often hear about did not happen to me. Although I began taking Ritalin and working with an organizational tutor, things didn't fall into place for quite a while. Lateness, being out of uniform, and missed work still plagued me. The frequency of my failure to abide by the school's expectations resulted in my removal from one of my sports teams and being denied participation in social activities. No matter how hard I tried, I never seemed to get control.

My parents were frustrated by my failure to change and my resistance to their help. Thinking the hard line approach would work, they grounded me. I missed out on a lot of fun. Their attempts to remind me about deadlines, cleaning my room, and wasting time seemed like constant nagging. Would they ever get off my back? No one seemed to realize that I was trying.

ADD has been a constant and painful struggle throughout my high school career, but now things are finally falling into place. My doctor switched my medication to Dexedrine, and it did wonders for me. Even after coming home late from playing in a basketball game, I was focused enough to do three hours of homework. My grades have also benefited. As I began to succeed in school, I felt better about myself and my potential to live a rewarding life. Challenges lie ahead with college and career, but I am confident now that my progress will continue.

◆ BRENDAN ◆

Having ADD is definitely not a day at the beach. Having ADD is a constant struggle that I will have to live with for the rest of my life. My name is Brendan and I have Attention Deficit Disorder. I am now attending high school as a freshman and thought it would be good to reflect on the various obstacles and freeways I have encountered in the past nine years.

In third grade I was diagnosed with ADD. Now let me tell you, this was not easy to cope with at such a young age, someone telling me I had some sort of disease! Once I found out I wasn't going to die, I felt a little relieved. Death crossed my mind many times as the process of using medication to treat my problems began. Since one medication is not the same for everybody, I went through months of ongoing trials of different dosages, types, and times of administration to make my symptoms disappear. Don't worry, I've been there.

As I reached fourth and fifth grade, I really started to struggle. Although my doctor had found the proper medication for me, I was denying that I needed it. For my parents it was a constant struggle to get me to take my medication. My mom even used to hide it in ice cream so I wouldn't find it, but I always would. At this age it was hard to accept the fact that I had a problem. Sixth, seventh, and eighth grades were about the same.

Entering high school as a freshman was when I turned around. I am still not sure whether it's the atmosphere of my particular school or if it's the idea of high school itself.

During the summer, I was required to go to summer school for math and English. I think that all the people at summer school had a learning disability, at least in my classes. But summer school was very good for me; it got me prepared for the upcoming school year. I also met some friends who would be in my class. My English teacher in summer school turned out to be my English teacher for the school year as well. Besides meeting new people and getting a head start on the upcoming work, I also got to know the school before any of the other freshman attending. I started playing football during the summer as well. I think it was playing a fall sport that set the stage for my improvement.

Every day during the school year, I would ride the bus home after a long football practice and arrive home about seven-thirty or eight. I would get home, shower, and then eat. I had no time for goofing off; I had to get my work done. I started to get tired of working so hard, so I told myself I would work my butt off until the first report card and see the results. The results blew me away. Of the six classes I was taking, I got five A's and one B, in art. This would get me First Honors. Last year, in elementary school, I had been getting C's and D's. This was the best report card I ever got in my life!

This is my success story. All my life I was convinced I would never succeed, but I was wrong. Just because you have ADD doesn't mean you can't accomplish anything. I'm proof of that, and if I can do it so can you!

◆ TOM ◆

At first everything seemed to be going fine. I had just entered my second year at a prep school and was doing reasonably well. Then, from late October to early December all hell broke loose. From my point of view, there are three things that dominate your life as a teen—education, parents, and social life.

When I fell apart in late October, it started a chain reaction that began with school, led to my parents, and then, because my parents were making me study all of the time, destroyed my social life to a huge degree. Neither I, nor anyone else, can figure out exactly what happened, but I do remember that one thing led to another. It really bothered me that I had a disability that made me have to work twice as hard as many other kids in my school to pull off not even A grades, but grades in the low 80's and high 70's. So at that point I just gave up and stopped putting in the effort and doing the work. My grades fell and I began to lie to my parents about the amount of homework that I had and the grades that I was receiving. Things got pretty bad, and for a while I thought that I might be asked to leave my school. But I pulled myself together with two weeks to go in the term and scored really well on all but one of my exams.

I've also got the rest of my life back on track in the months since all of this happened. I've tried to avoid falling behind again, and I now have a tutor who comes three times a week to help me keep on track. The point of my telling you this is that the same thing could, and might already, have happened to you. If there's any lesson I've learned from my experience, it's that life may be unfair, but that isn't a reason to stop trying, because if you do, life will just get more unfair and you will end up more miserable.

◆ JESSE ◆

I'm a student who recently transferred from a smaller private school to a larger public high school, and, contrary to what most people say, it was the best move for me. I had been in my previous school since kindergarten. I had never done very well and did not feel at all smart compared to the other kids. I stopped working and putting in the effort since I was doing poorly anyway. By seventh grade I was really feeling bad about myself and was diagnosed as being depressed. My doctor started me on Prozac in addition to my Dexedrine. That was when we also decided that it would be a good idea for me to switch schools.

In public school I had more flexibility and became better organized. I used my time differently. Each day at lunch I would meet with another student from my math class, and we would go over the work together. I also used my study hall to complete the major portion of my homework. I had less work to do at night and my parents were not always on me to study. My grades improved and I made second honor roll for the first time in my life. I became more interested in learning and asking for help when I needed it. I am tutored in geometry before each test and have an organizational tutor once a week. In looking back I feel it was the combination of the Prozac and my renewed effort that made all of the difference. I can't urge other kids enough to continue to look for solutions to your problems and not to give up. I'm sure glad I didn't.

◆ EMELINE ◆

Hi. My name is Emeline. I am 13 years old and go to middle school. I have ADD and my brother has ADHD. My brother Erik and I both take medication. (By the way, my brother is nine years old and in the fourth grade.) Part of having ADD is being disorganized, but my brother and I have found many things that help with this problem.

On Fridays or Saturdays I clean out my notebook and clean my room. This keeps me organized during school, and I'm not always losing things like homework, reports, essays, and so on. My brother and I also set out our clothes the night before school and make sure that we have everything packed up for school for the next day, like putting our homework in our notebook or in a safe place where we know we will find it when we need it. Because missing assignments were also a problem for me, I now make sure to copy my homework in an assignment book right when I receive it. By doing these few simple things, I have managed to stay on the honor roll for two years straight! And I am sure you can too! Life with ADD doesn't need to be complicated or a hassle, you just need to take the time to figure out what works for you to overcome some of the common problems.

◆ SHANNON ◆

I think of my middle school years as some of the best times in my life. You're past all the elementary students but not yet old enough to face the harder complications of high school. You meet all kinds of new people and take on new classes. You find out who you are.

I was diagnosed with ADD in the beginning of the seventh grade, and I thought my life was over. It was hard enough to try to fit in, you know, to be accepted, and I didn't want to be different. I thought that being ADD would show. I thought that maybe I was diagnosed wrong, and I thought that this just couldn't be me. I couldn't relate it to my life. I thought it was a big mistake.

I was put on Ritalin right away, and daily trips to the nurse's office after lunch became routine. My parents made me begin math tutoring after school once a week. Math was never my favorite subject and up to this day I still despise it. At first I hated the idea of being tutored because I felt that I could do it fine on my own. But now I see that it really helps me. Sometimes I really won't get it in class. But if someone just sits down and explains it to me more, then I will get it. It's just something that I have learned to accept about myself.

Throughout most of my seventh grade year, I was very unhappy about being ADD. I started on time-released medication so that I wouldn't have to go to the nurse's office. I just wanted to be like my friends. I felt like I was less intelligent and it really bothered me.

Then in the eighth grade I met Joe. Since we rode the same bus, we became friends. Not long after, I found out that he, too, was ADD. I thought about what a neat person he was, fun to talk to, creative and popular. You would never know he was ADD! I began to realize that this was common and that I was not alone.

Now I won't let it hold me back. I am a committed dancer and writer. I take high school Spanish I and Honors English. I have been on the Student Council for two years. I love art and music. There are many, many things that I can do, but I also realize the things that I struggle with.

A lot of times I need extra time on tests. I just go into the counselor's office, finish it, then return it to the teacher. No big deal. I'm allowed to use a calculator in my physical science class so that I won't make silly little errors in the math and have it mess up the whole equation. I feel a lot better now. I understand what I can do to help myself do better.

The best thing to do is to ask questions when you need to. That's what your teachers are there for. Make them do their job! Take extra time if you need it. Seek extra help. Do whatever you can to help yourself understand. You can do it! Most of all, you need to realize that ADD is a part of you, and you have to accept it. Just try to be the best you can be and that will be enough.

◆ STUART ◆

My study habits were instilled at a small private boarding school which focused on discipline and study habits for LD boys. They had mandatory study halls for most of the day, with barely any chance for distraction. My eighth grade year, I spent two hours every night locked up in a proctored study hall with nothing but my books. Goofing off was not an issue. There was nothing to do but homework, so that's what I did.

I spent my ninth grade year there, too. Ninth graders were allowed to do their homework in their own rooms, to prepare us for a normal secondary school. I had an advantage: I was a prefect in a separate dorm, so during study hall I was alone in a small dorm with no foreign noises for distraction. Had I spent the year in the ninth grade dorm with the rest of the ninth graders, I doubt I would have gotten as much work done. After two years of this institutional routine, I went to another private boarding high school.

In many aspects, high school was not very different from what I had experienced previously. Freshmen and sophomores had to spend the evening study hall in their rooms. I could not do any work in this atmosphere because the kids on my floor were not interested in work at all. They spent study hall mostly eating pizza and playing soccer in the hall. I explained my dilemma to my dorm head, and he said I could go to the library, where there is no talking.

The library was where I got all my work done for the next two and a half years. It was the perfect environment, and the only environment where I could get my work done. It was quiet, I was used to the view, and there were no distractions. Once I established my working area, I could get a lot of work done without the distractions that a dorm had.

The basic desire to do well and stay organized that I learned over the years has stayed with me, but I really cannot get any decent work done without Ritalin.

So much for my experience with LD and ADD at boarding school. I hope that if it's what you are looking for, you will investigate one of the several boarding schools around the country that specialize in LD or ADD.

◆ CARLOS ◆

My experience at a boarding school has been extremely positive. This year was my third year attending a boarding school. From my personal experience, I think that I accomplished a lot, raising my grades to all A's and B's. The jump in academic standings was mostly due to the fact that I really decided to take it upon myself to complete my work and try my hardest. The teachers were wonderful about helping me learn about new study skills. The school's extremely structured program was one of the main reasons for my success. There was never a chance for me to become distracted from my studies. The main aspect that affected me was monitored study halls. The result of having these study halls and learning how to effectively use them was that I completed my work—something that I never had done before. Once I had done the work, I would look it over and sometimes go and get help from teachers, all of whom lived on campus and were always available. As a result of this, the only thing that I could possibly do was study.

The responsibility of taking care of myself and learning how to live on my own was all part of boarding, too. After two years of boarding school, I changed a great deal. The boarding school life introduced me to many kids and adults who influenced me a great deal.

My next big leap in my educational experience involved transferring to another boarding school. This school gives the students a great deal of freedom. A few times during the day you might have to check in with a teacher or sign in, but for the most part you're completely free. This freedom was a serious problem for me in the beginning. Still being used to the coat-and-tie strictness of my previous school, it was easy for me to become corrupt in the free environment. After a few weeks I started to realize that I was extremely unorganized and that I had poor time management, so I took it upon myself to become organized. By using all of the study skills I had learned previously, I slowly started to adapt them to my life.

However, my efficiency was extremely affected by my two roommates, who didn't concern themselves about work. My roommates were extremely social, and both had never been to boarding school. As they were learning about how to adjust, they still were extremely distracting. We all ended up making a mutual agreement that our parents would kill us if our grades were poor, so they quickly learned to do their work.

However, the main problem that I had was that I tend to do my work a little slower than most people. I usually stay up until 11:30 checking my work, which causes a major problem when you have roommates who want to get some sleep. Another problem was when one of my roommates would have little or no work to do. All three of us had computers, and they were the next main distraction. Computer games were my academic life's worst enemy. I ended up having to erase every single game on my computer so that I wouldn't waste time. All of these decisions were of my own choice.

After a term I understood a little more how to organize my time and to fully take responsibility for my actions. In order to study I had to go to the library and find myself a little desk on which to work. However, once 9:30 came and I had to leave the library, it was virtually impossible to do my homework in my room. Overall I think that my experience at boarding schools was a success and that I accomplished a lot. I developed in many ways, and I feel that I am presently better off than I would be if I had stayed at my local schools.

9.

ADVOCATING FOR YOURSELF

To effectively deal with your ADD, it is important that you gain both an awareness of your strengths and weaknesses and the skills necessary to be an advocate for yourself. After learning more about your ADD and the accommodations and strategies that make learning and day-to-day activities easier for you, it is important to be able to articulate your needs to others. After all, they are YOUR problems. You are the one who has to live with them. We all hope that your parents are not going to go away to college with you. So, you need to take charge now. High school is a good time to try out strategies and practice speaking up for yourself. But how do you talk to teachers and get your needs met?

The rights of all students with disabilities are protected by several laws designed to assure equal education for all. Attention deficit disorder is considered a disability under federal law when it substantially limits a major life activity such as learning or working.

Individuals with ADD are guaranteed free and appropriate public education by three federal laws. These laws are the Individuals with Disabilities Education Act of 1990 (IDEA), Section 504 of the Rehabilitation Act of 1973 (RA), and the Americans with Disabilities Act of 1990 (ADA).

After testing the student, the school system will determine whether he or she is eligible under the law to be considered for services and accommodations. If found eligible, the school system must design an educational program to meet the student's unique needs. This program is termed an Individualized Education Program, or IEP. The development of an IEP requires the participation of a team of individuals. This team should include the parents, the student (when appropriate), the classroom teacher, designated specialists, and a representative of the public agency qualified to provide special services. Now is the time to begin to get involved in this process. Ask to attend meetings that are held to discuss your program or IEP development. Make sure that you speak up about what you want and what works for you.

Section 504 of the Rehabilitation Act, like IDEA, requires that schools that receive federal funds address the needs of students with disabilities. There is, however, an important difference between these two laws. While IDEA requires that a student have a disability that requires special education services, Section 504 qualifies a person on the basis of having an impairment that limits one of life's major activities, including learning. A student with ADD who does not need special education services under IDEA may by qualified to receive accommodations under Section 504 of the RA.

A student who qualifies under the RA can then have a 504 ACCOMMODATION PLAN drawn up at school to serve his or her needs. Most school systems elect to deal with this process at the local school level. Teams are set up to determine the individual student's need within that environment and to create the 504 Accommodation Plan. The plan assures that all parties involved are aware of the needs of a particular student, and of what must be done to address them. Successful accommodation plans usually undertake to match a solution to a particular need. These solutions are usually easy to implement and relatively inexpensive. They do, however, require flexibility on the part of the student and the teacher and sometimes a creative problem-solving approach.

In order to help you better understand its design and usefulness, a sample 504 Accommodation Plan is shown on the next page. You will need to individualize your Accommodation Plan to fit your unique needs. Not all students will need all or many of the sample accommodations. Pick those that you think will be of benefit to you and write up a sample 504 Accommodation Plan. Your school may have other sample plans for you to look at.

The accommodations in the sample plan are certainly not all-inclusive. They are merely examples of the kinds of accommodations that benefit the student with attention deficits. All of these accomodations can be addressed easily within the regular educational setting.

SAMPLE 504 ACCOMMODATION PLAN

It has been determined that _____(Name of student)_____

School: Date of Birth:

Teacher: Grade:

qualifies as a handicapped individual under Section 504 of the Rehabilitation Act of 1973 and the following *Areas of Need* have been established:

A. distractibility

B. missing assignments

C. poor handwriting

D. inability to sit for long periods

E. calling out behavior

F. poor test performance

Accommodations agreed upon by the school to meet these individual needs in accordance with Section 504 guidelines are:

A. 1. Preferential seating/near the teacher or away from distracting stimuli such as doors and windows.

    2. Cue the student to remain on task.

    3. Stand near the student to give directions or lightly touch the student on the shoulder to refocus.

B. 1. Assign a homework buddy.

    2. Provide a copy of all assignments in writing.

    3. Provide a weekly or monthly syllabus.

    4. Conduct a weekly assignment completion check up.

C. 1. Allow computer or typewritten assignments.

2. Shorten assignments or break them down into smaller segments.

3. Give extra time to complete written assignments.

D. 1. Give frequent breaks.

2. Allow movement within the classroom.

3. Assign the student tasks that will allow for walking around inside the class or out.

E. 1. Institute a behavior management program.

2. Reward appropriate behavior.

F. 1. Give untimed tests if necessary.

2. Require fewer correct responses to achieve a grade or allow more objective answers rather than long essays.

3. Give part or all of the test orally.

4. Give frequent short quizzes and avoid long exams.

5. Read test items to the student.

6. Allow open book tests.

7. Give take-home tests or extracredit material.

8. Allow the student to record answers on a tape recorder.

Participants present at development of PLAN:

Parent's signature:

Student's signature (when appropriate):

Case manager: Date:

Several of these examples are appropriate for all students, but others may be more or less useful according to the age of the student and the classroom setting. However, in order for accommodations to be successful, they must be applied consistently, and it is here that the difficulty lies in many instances. You must both seek accommodations and take advantage of them when they are offered.

How do you get the teachers to respond to your needs? Being honest about your needs up front helps. This means discussing strengths and weaknesses at the beginning of the semester rather than approaching the teacher only when problems arise or when you are asking for an exemption. Remember, having ADD should never be an excuse for not doing what is required or expected. By conveying to the teacher early that your only reason for requesting these accommodations is to do well and show what you are capable of learning, you are more likely to receive requested accommodations.

CONCLUSION

The fact that you have been diagnosed with a disorder does not mean that you now have an "excuse" or a "cop out" not to be the best you can be. Students with ADD should be encouraged to do their best and to perform up to their abilities despite any disabilities that they may have. Following is some advice from other students with ADD regarding this topic and ADD in general.

Lori ◆ Believe in yourself!

John ◆ Don't feel bad when teachers criticize you. You should go to them first and tell that you have problems paying attention and that you would like them to learn more about ADD.

Sean ◆ It's not that bad having ADD. I have lots of energy to keep going, and that really helps when I play sports such as hockey or soccer.

Patrick ◆ It is your responsibility to make your teachers more aware of your ADD.

James ◆ ADD is not an excuse for your behavior.

Colin ◆ You are smarter than you think. Just because things are harder for you, that doesn't mean that you're stupid.

Matthew ◆ Be sure to block out distractions and DECIDE to pay attention to what is important.

George ◆ It may take longer but you CAN learn more information and go farther than others.

Peter ◆ Think of ADD as an ADDvantage.

Johann ◆ It's great! With ADD you can usually do two things at the same time.

Kellie ◆ Be yourself and don't care about what other people say.

Caitlin ◆ Kids with ADD are interested in more things and are more interesting than others.

Jimmy ◆ Don't blame everything on your ADD.

Some good advice, but how do you keep from getting down on yourself? First, it is important to set realistic goals. Be honest about your strengths and weaknesses. If you are not good at math, don't set a goal of majoring in engineering. Be open to looking at related fields that may interest you as much and that may be more in line with your abilities.

Don't try to solve all of your problems at one time. Dealing with issues individually makes them more manageable and allows you the time to think through to more creative solutions. Tackling academic or organizational problems that are daily stumbling blocks and consume so much energy may free some time to work on friendships or improve relationships with your parents. Those, too, are areas of life that need to be nurtured.

In the summer perhaps you and your parents can relax from worries about your academic success. This might be a good time to address other concerns. Enlist the help of a therapist, if necessary, in order to get started. Try dealing with less threatening issues first and then move on to the bigger and more inflammatory ones that seem to arise over and over. Not all problems will be resolved on the first try, but it is important to make some steps in the right direction. It is also okay to resolve disagreements by agreeing to disagree, as long as you do so with respect for the other person and without anger and hostility.

Be sure to ask for help when you need it. There are lots of people out there who are willing to help. They include therapists, counselors, coaches, religious leaders, teachers, your parents, older siblings, grandparents, and neighbors—to name just a few. You may also want to join or start a support group for teens with ADD. Having someone to talk to who understands your problems is always useful.

In my practice, I find that during their early teen years, many kids find it difficult to admit that there is something "wrong" with them. They see the diagnosis of ADD as criticism from parents or other adults and as a failure on their part. It is important to talk about these feelings and to deal with the realities of having ADD. It certainly doesn't go away by itself and denying it may only make things worse.

Be sure to concentrate on the positive. There are lots of good things about having ADD, and you have many positive qualities. Write them down in a diary or journal or on a piece of paper. Seeing them in print will make them more real for you. You can destroy the paper once you are finished or better yet, put it away in a drawer to be pulled out again when you need to feel better about yourself. We all have bad days that could use some cheering up.

In the end, with all of the necessary supports, adolescents with ADD can be successful. Now more than ever, you have many opportunities available to you to display your talents and gifts. You may look to continue your education at the college level, if that is what you choose to do, or enter the workplace assured that with the proper accommodations you can be productive in the pursuit of your dreams and goals. Knowledge about ADD and how to deal effectively with its symptoms will allow you to enter into adulthood confident in your abilities and aware of your strengths.

Good luck to all of you now and in the years ahead!

RESOURCES

Other books and resources to turn to for help

Bringing Up Parents: The Teenager's Handbook by Alex J. Parker. Free Spirit Publishing, 800-735-7323, 276 pages, $12.95. Ages 13 and up. Specific suggestions for teenagers on how to resolve conflicts with parents, accept responsibility, and create a happier home environment.

Get off My Brain: Survival Guide for Lazy Students by Randall McCutcheon. Free Spirit Publishing, 800-735-7323, 120 pages, $8.95. For ages 15 and up. A creative study guide that offers ways to succeed in school and combine "laughs with learning."

I Would If I Could: A Teenager's Guide to ADHD/Hyperactivity by Michael Gordon. GSI Publications, 315-446-4849, 34 pages, $12.50. This book provides information about ADHD and explores its impact on the life of a teenager, his parents, self-esteem, and friendships.

Making the Grade: An Adolescent's Struggle with ADD by Roberta Parker. Available from A.D.D. Warehouse, 800-233-9273, 47 pages, $10.00. For kids 9 to 14, this book tells the story of a junior high student who, once diagnosed with ADD, learns how to help himself.

Putting on the Brakes: Young People's Guide to Understanding Attention Deficit Hyperactivity Disorder (ADHD) by Patricia O. Quinn and Judith M. Stern. Magination Press, 800-825-3089, 64 pages, $8.95. Although this book was written for 8 to 13 year olds, it provides a great deal of information and background on ADHD. Many adults have said that they found it useful and easy to read in one sitting.

School Strategies for ADD Teens by Kathleen Nadeau, Ellen Dixon, and Susan Biggs. Chesapeake Psychological Publications, 703-642-6697. This booklet provides suggestions for parents, counselors, and teachers, as well as middle and high school students with ADD, for improved classroom performance.

◆ ◆ ◆

These books will help you prepare for college

ADD and the College Student edited by Patricia O. Quinn. Magination Press, 1-800-825-3089, 112 pages, $13.95. This book is perfect for juniors and seniors in high school as they prepare for college. It provides information on choosing a college, discusses what to expect during senior year, and presents accommodations and tips for success at the college level.

The K & W Guide to Colleges for the Learning Disabled, edited by Marybeth Kravets and Imy F. Wax. New York: HarperCollins, 800-331-3761, 592 pages, $20.00.

Peterson's Guide to Colleges with Programs for Students with Learning Disabilities, edited by Charles T. Mangrum, III and Stephen S. Strichart. Princeton, NJ: Petersons Guides, 800-338-3282, 672 pages, $24.95.

Survival Guide for College Students with ADD or LD by Kathleen Nadeau. Magination Press, 800-825-3089, 56 pages, $9.95. This book provides many valuable suggestions on how students can help themselves once they get to college.

Unlocking Potential: College and Other Choices for Learning Disabled People—A Step-by-Step Guide, by Barbara Scheiber and Jeanne Talpers. Chevy Chase, MD: Adler & Adler, 301-654-4271, 195 pages, $12.95.

◆ ◆ ◆

Here are some books you might recommend to your parents

Surviving Your Adolescents by Thomas Phelan. Child Management, Inc., 800-442-4453, 136 pages, $12.95. Provides a step-by-step approach to deal with adolescents and offers concrete solutions to many of the problems commonly encountered.

Teenagers with ADD: A Parents' Guide by Chris Dendy. Woodbine House, 800-843-7323, 400 pages, $16.95. This book provides practical advice and information on ADD. Has a review of the literature, glossary of terms, and a resource list to help teens with ADD succeed.

ABOUT THE AUTHOR

◆ ◆ ◆

Patricia O. Quinn, M.D., is a developmental pediatrician practicing in the Washington, D.C. area. She specializes in child development and psychopharmacology, and works extensively in the areas of ADD, learning disabilities, and mental retardation. She gives workshops and has published widely in these fields. She is also the editor of *ADD and the College Student: A Guide for High School and College Students with Attention Deficit Disorder*; co-author of *Putting on the Brakes: Young People's Guide to Understanding Attention Deficit Hyperactivity Disorder* and *The "Putting on the Brakes" Activity Book for Young People with ADHD*; and co-editor of *BRAKES: The Interactive Newsletter for Kids with ADD*.